50 Premium Chicken Recipes

By: Kelly Johnson

Table of Contents

- Herb-Roasted Chicken with Lemon
- Chicken Piccata with Capers and Lemon Butter Sauce
- Chicken Marsala with Mushrooms
- Honey Garlic Chicken Thighs
- Chicken Alfredo with Fettuccine
- Spicy Korean Chicken Wings
- Moroccan Chicken Tagine with Apricots
- Chicken Tikka Masala
- Grilled Lemon and Rosemary Chicken
- Chicken Enchiladas with Green Sauce
- Balsamic Glazed Chicken Breasts
- Coconut Curry Chicken
- Chicken and Mushroom Risotto
- Garlic Butter Chicken with Asparagus
- Chicken Shawarma with Tahini Sauce
- Chicken Parmesan with Marinara and Mozzarella
- Teriyaki Chicken Stir-Fry
- BBQ Chicken Pizza
- Chicken Fricassée with Vegetables
- Crispy Chicken Thighs with Garlic and Herbs
- Chicken Kiev with Herb Butter
- Spinach and Feta Stuffed Chicken Breasts
- Chicken and Waffles with Maple Syrup
- Lemon-Dill Chicken Skewers
- Chicken and Sausage Gumbo
- Pesto Chicken Pasta Salad
- Chicken Cacciatore with Bell Peppers
- Sesame Chicken with Broccoli
- Stuffed Chicken Breasts with Sun-Dried Tomatoes
- Chicken and Vegetable Stir-Fry
- Chipotle Chicken Burrito Bowl
- Thai Basil Chicken
- Creamy Tuscan Chicken
- Buttermilk Fried Chicken
- Chicken Pot Pie with Flaky Crust

- Maple-Mustard Glazed Chicken
- Chicken Roulade with Spinach and Ricotta
- Chicken Caesar Salad with Homemade Dressing
- Garlic Parmesan Chicken Wings
- Chicken and Spinach Stuffed Shells
- Cajun Chicken Pasta
- Chicken and Broccoli Alfredo Bake
- Lemon Garlic Herb Chicken Thighs
- Chicken Fajitas with Peppers and Onions
- Thai Chicken Satay with Peanut Sauce
- Chipotle Lime Grilled Chicken
- Orange-Glazed Chicken with Sesame Seeds
- Chicken and Quinoa Salad with Avocado
- Chicken Stroganoff with Egg Noodles
- Garlic and Herb Grilled Chicken Breasts

Herb-Roasted Chicken with Lemon

Ingredients:

- 1 whole chicken (about 4-5 lbs)
- 2 lemons, quartered
- 4 cloves garlic, minced
- 2 tablespoons olive oil
- 1 tablespoon fresh rosemary, chopped
- 1 tablespoon fresh thyme, chopped
- Salt and pepper to taste

Instructions:

1. Preheat the oven to 425°F (220°C).
2. In a bowl, mix olive oil, garlic, rosemary, thyme, salt, and pepper.
3. Rub the mixture all over the chicken, including under the skin.
4. Stuff the cavity with lemon quarters.
5. Roast in the oven for 1 hour and 15 minutes or until the internal temperature reaches 165°F (74°C).

Chicken Piccata with Capers and Lemon Butter Sauce

Ingredients:

- 4 boneless, skinless chicken breasts
- 1/2 cup flour
- 1/4 cup olive oil
- 1/4 cup lemon juice
- 1/4 cup chicken broth
- 2 tablespoons capers, rinsed
- 4 tablespoons butter
- Salt and pepper to taste

Instructions:

1. Season chicken with salt and pepper, then dredge in flour.
2. In a skillet, heat olive oil over medium heat and cook chicken until golden brown on both sides.
3. Remove chicken and add lemon juice, chicken broth, and capers to the pan.
4. Simmer for 2-3 minutes, then whisk in butter until melted.
5. Return chicken to the skillet, cooking for an additional 2 minutes before serving.

Chicken Marsala with Mushrooms

Ingredients:

- 4 boneless, skinless chicken breasts
- 1/2 cup flour
- 2 tablespoons olive oil
- 8 oz mushrooms, sliced
- 1 cup Marsala wine
- 1 cup chicken broth
- 2 tablespoons butter
- Salt and pepper to taste

Instructions:

1. Season chicken with salt and pepper, then dredge in flour.
2. In a skillet, heat olive oil and cook chicken until golden brown, then remove.
3. Add mushrooms to the pan and sauté until softened.
4. Pour in Marsala wine and chicken broth, scraping up any browned bits.
5. Return chicken to the skillet and simmer for 10 minutes, then stir in butter before serving.

Honey Garlic Chicken Thighs

Ingredients:

- 6 chicken thighs, skin-on and bone-in
- 1/3 cup honey
- 1/4 cup soy sauce
- 4 cloves garlic, minced
- 1 tablespoon olive oil
- Salt and pepper to taste

Instructions:

1. Preheat the oven to 400°F (200°C).
2. In a bowl, whisk together honey, soy sauce, garlic, olive oil, salt, and pepper.
3. Place chicken thighs in a baking dish and pour sauce over them.
4. Bake for 35-40 minutes until the chicken is cooked through and caramelized.

Chicken Alfredo with Fettuccine

Ingredients:

- 8 oz fettuccine pasta
- 2 tablespoons butter
- 2 cloves garlic, minced
- 1 cup heavy cream
- 1 cup grated Parmesan cheese
- 2 boneless, skinless chicken breasts, cooked and sliced
- Salt and pepper to taste

Instructions:

1. Cook fettuccine according to package instructions; drain.
2. In a skillet, melt butter over medium heat and sauté garlic until fragrant.
3. Add heavy cream and bring to a simmer, then stir in Parmesan cheese until smooth.
4. Add cooked fettuccine and chicken, tossing to combine. Season with salt and pepper before serving.

Spicy Korean Chicken Wings

Ingredients:

- 2 lbs chicken wings
- 1/4 cup gochujang (Korean chili paste)
- 2 tablespoons soy sauce
- 2 tablespoons honey
- 1 tablespoon sesame oil
- 2 cloves garlic, minced
- Sesame seeds for garnish

Instructions:

1. Preheat the oven to 425°F (220°C).
2. In a bowl, mix gochujang, soy sauce, honey, sesame oil, and garlic.
3. Toss chicken wings in the sauce until well coated.
4. Arrange on a baking sheet and bake for 30-35 minutes, flipping halfway through.
5. Garnish with sesame seeds before serving.

Moroccan Chicken Tagine with Apricots

Ingredients:

- 4 chicken thighs
- 2 tablespoons olive oil
- 1 onion, chopped
- 2 cloves garlic, minced
- 1 teaspoon ground cumin
- 1 teaspoon ground cinnamon
- 1 teaspoon paprika
- 1/2 cup dried apricots, chopped
- 1 cup chicken broth
- Salt and pepper to taste

Instructions:

1. In a large pot, heat olive oil and sauté onion and garlic until softened.
2. Add chicken and brown on all sides.
3. Stir in spices, apricots, and chicken broth.
4. Simmer for 30-35 minutes until chicken is cooked through.

Chicken Tikka Masala

Ingredients:

- 1 lb boneless, skinless chicken breasts, cubed
- 1 cup plain yogurt
- 2 tablespoons tikka masala spice blend
- 1 onion, chopped
- 4 cloves garlic, minced
- 1 can (14 oz) crushed tomatoes
- 1/2 cup heavy cream
- Fresh cilantro for garnish

Instructions:

1. Marinate chicken in yogurt and tikka masala for at least 1 hour.
2. In a skillet, sauté onion and garlic until fragrant.
3. Add marinated chicken and cook until browned.
4. Stir in crushed tomatoes and simmer for 15 minutes.
5. Stir in heavy cream and garnish with cilantro before serving.

Grilled Lemon and Rosemary Chicken

Ingredients:

- 4 boneless, skinless chicken breasts
- 1/4 cup olive oil
- 2 lemons, juiced and zested
- 3 cloves garlic, minced
- 2 tablespoons fresh rosemary, chopped
- Salt and pepper to taste

Instructions:

1. In a bowl, whisk together olive oil, lemon juice, lemon zest, garlic, rosemary, salt, and pepper.
2. Add chicken breasts to the marinade and let sit for at least 30 minutes.
3. Preheat the grill to medium-high heat.
4. Grill chicken for 6-7 minutes on each side, or until cooked through.

Chicken Enchiladas with Green Sauce

Ingredients:

- 2 cups shredded cooked chicken
- 8 corn tortillas
- 2 cups green enchilada sauce
- 1 cup shredded cheese (cheddar or Monterey Jack)
- 1/2 cup sour cream
- Chopped cilantro for garnish

Instructions:

1. Preheat oven to 350°F (175°C).
2. In a skillet, heat 1 cup of green sauce.
3. Warm tortillas in the microwave until pliable.
4. Fill each tortilla with chicken, roll up, and place seam-side down in a baking dish.
5. Pour remaining sauce over enchiladas and sprinkle with cheese.
6. Bake for 20 minutes, then serve with sour cream and cilantro.

Balsamic Glazed Chicken Breasts

Ingredients:

- 4 boneless, skinless chicken breasts
- 1/2 cup balsamic vinegar
- 1/4 cup honey
- 2 cloves garlic, minced
- 1 tablespoon olive oil
- Salt and pepper to taste

Instructions:

1. In a bowl, mix balsamic vinegar, honey, garlic, olive oil, salt, and pepper.
2. Marinate chicken in the mixture for at least 30 minutes.
3. Preheat a skillet over medium heat and cook chicken for 5-7 minutes on each side until cooked through.
4. Drizzle with leftover marinade during the last few minutes of cooking.

Coconut Curry Chicken

Ingredients:

- 1 lb boneless, skinless chicken thighs, cubed
- 1 can (14 oz) coconut milk
- 2 tablespoons curry powder
- 1 onion, chopped
- 3 cloves garlic, minced
- 1 tablespoon ginger, minced
- 2 cups spinach
- Salt to taste

Instructions:

1. In a skillet, sauté onion, garlic, and ginger until fragrant.
2. Add chicken and cook until browned.
3. Stir in coconut milk and curry powder, simmer for 15 minutes.
4. Add spinach and cook until wilted. Season with salt before serving.

Chicken and Mushroom Risotto

Ingredients:

- 1 cup Arborio rice
- 4 cups chicken broth
- 1 cup cooked chicken, shredded
- 1 cup mushrooms, sliced
- 1 onion, chopped
- 1/2 cup Parmesan cheese, grated
- 2 tablespoons butter
- Salt and pepper to taste

Instructions:

1. In a pot, heat chicken broth until simmering.
2. In a separate pan, melt butter and sauté onion and mushrooms until softened.
3. Add Arborio rice and cook for 1-2 minutes.
4. Gradually add broth, stirring continuously, until absorbed.
5. Stir in chicken and Parmesan cheese, season with salt and pepper before serving.

Garlic Butter Chicken with Asparagus

Ingredients:

- 4 boneless, skinless chicken thighs
- 1 bunch asparagus, trimmed
- 4 tablespoons butter
- 4 cloves garlic, minced
- Salt and pepper to taste

Instructions:

1. In a skillet, melt 2 tablespoons of butter and cook chicken for 5-7 minutes on each side until golden brown.
2. Remove chicken and set aside.
3. In the same skillet, add remaining butter and garlic, then asparagus.
4. Sauté until asparagus is tender.
5. Return chicken to the skillet, season with salt and pepper, and cook for another 2 minutes.

Chicken Shawarma with Tahini Sauce

Ingredients:

- 1 lb boneless, skinless chicken thighs
- 2 tablespoons shawarma spice blend
- 3 tablespoons olive oil
- 1/4 cup tahini
- 2 tablespoons lemon juice
- Salt to taste
- Pita bread and veggies for serving

Instructions:

1. In a bowl, mix chicken with shawarma spice, olive oil, and salt.
2. Marinate for at least 1 hour, then grill or pan-fry until cooked through.
3. For the tahini sauce, whisk together tahini, lemon juice, and salt.
4. Serve chicken in pita bread with tahini sauce and veggies.

Chicken Parmesan with Marinara and Mozzarella

Ingredients:

- 4 boneless, skinless chicken breasts
- 1 cup breadcrumbs
- 1/2 cup Parmesan cheese, grated
- 2 cups marinara sauce
- 1 cup mozzarella cheese, shredded
- Olive oil for frying
- Salt and pepper to taste

Instructions:

1. Preheat oven to 375°F (190°C).
2. Mix breadcrumbs and Parmesan cheese.
3. Season chicken with salt and pepper, then coat with breadcrumb mixture.
4. In a skillet, heat olive oil and fry chicken until golden on both sides.
5. Place chicken in a baking dish, top with marinara sauce and mozzarella cheese, then bake for 20 minutes until cheese is bubbly.

Teriyaki Chicken Stir-Fry

Ingredients:

- 1 lb boneless, skinless chicken breasts, sliced
- 2 cups mixed vegetables (bell peppers, broccoli, snap peas)
- 1/2 cup teriyaki sauce
- 2 tablespoons vegetable oil
- Cooked rice for serving

Instructions:

1. In a large skillet or wok, heat vegetable oil over medium-high heat.
2. Add sliced chicken and cook until browned.
3. Add mixed vegetables and stir-fry for 3-4 minutes.
4. Pour in teriyaki sauce and cook for an additional 2-3 minutes until heated through.
5. Serve over cooked rice.

BBQ Chicken Pizza

Ingredients:

- 1 pre-made pizza crust
- 1 cup cooked chicken, shredded
- 1/2 cup BBQ sauce
- 1 cup shredded mozzarella cheese
- 1/2 red onion, thinly sliced
- 1/4 cup cilantro, chopped

Instructions:

1. Preheat the oven according to pizza crust instructions.
2. In a bowl, mix shredded chicken with BBQ sauce.
3. Spread the chicken mixture over the pizza crust.
4. Top with mozzarella cheese and red onion slices.
5. Bake according to crust instructions or until cheese is melted.
6. Garnish with chopped cilantro before serving.

Chicken Fricassée with Vegetables

Ingredients:

- 4 chicken thighs, skin-on
- 1 onion, chopped
- 2 carrots, sliced
- 2 celery stalks, sliced
- 2 cups chicken broth
- 1 cup heavy cream
- 2 tablespoons flour
- Salt and pepper to taste
- Fresh parsley for garnish

Instructions:

1. In a large skillet, brown chicken thighs on both sides.
2. Remove chicken and sauté onion, carrots, and celery until softened.
3. Stir in flour, then add chicken broth and bring to a simmer.
4. Return chicken to the skillet, cover, and cook for 30 minutes.
5. Stir in heavy cream, season with salt and pepper, and simmer for an additional 10 minutes.
6. Garnish with fresh parsley before serving.

Crispy Chicken Thighs with Garlic and Herbs

Ingredients:

- 4 chicken thighs, bone-in and skin-on
- 4 cloves garlic, minced
- 2 tablespoons fresh thyme, chopped
- 2 tablespoons olive oil
- Salt and pepper to taste

Instructions:

1. Preheat oven to 425°F (220°C).
2. In a bowl, mix garlic, thyme, olive oil, salt, and pepper.
3. Rub the mixture all over the chicken thighs.
4. Place chicken on a baking sheet and roast for 35-40 minutes until skin is crispy and chicken is cooked through.

Chicken Kiev with Herb Butter

Ingredients:

- 4 boneless, skinless chicken breasts
- 1/2 cup unsalted butter, softened
- 2 tablespoons fresh parsley, chopped
- 2 cloves garlic, minced
- 1/2 cup breadcrumbs
- Salt and pepper to taste

Instructions:

1. Preheat oven to 375°F (190°C).
2. In a bowl, mix butter, parsley, garlic, salt, and pepper.
3. Carefully cut a pocket into each chicken breast and fill with herb butter.
4. Dip chicken in breadcrumbs and place in a baking dish.
5. Bake for 25-30 minutes until chicken is cooked through and golden.

Spinach and Feta Stuffed Chicken Breasts

Ingredients:

- 4 boneless, skinless chicken breasts
- 1 cup fresh spinach, chopped
- 1/2 cup feta cheese, crumbled
- 1/4 cup cream cheese, softened
- 1 tablespoon olive oil
- Salt and pepper to taste

Instructions:

1. Preheat oven to 375°F (190°C).
2. In a bowl, combine spinach, feta, cream cheese, salt, and pepper.
3. Cut a pocket into each chicken breast and stuff with the spinach mixture.
4. Heat olive oil in a skillet and sear chicken on both sides.
5. Transfer to a baking dish and bake for 25-30 minutes until cooked through.

Chicken and Waffles with Maple Syrup

Ingredients:

- 4 chicken thighs, fried
- 4 waffles, toasted
- Maple syrup for drizzling
- Butter for serving

Instructions:

1. Prepare waffles according to package instructions.
2. Fry chicken thighs until crispy and cooked through.
3. Serve fried chicken on top of waffles with butter and drizzle with maple syrup.

Lemon-Dill Chicken Skewers

Ingredients:

- 1 lb boneless, skinless chicken breasts, cubed
- 1/4 cup olive oil
- Juice of 2 lemons
- 2 tablespoons fresh dill, chopped
- Salt and pepper to taste
- Skewers (if using wooden skewers, soak in water for 30 minutes)

Instructions:

1. In a bowl, whisk together olive oil, lemon juice, dill, salt, and pepper.
2. Add chicken cubes and marinate for at least 30 minutes.
3. Thread chicken onto skewers and grill over medium heat for 10-12 minutes, turning occasionally until cooked through.

Chicken and Sausage Gumbo

Ingredients:

- 1 lb boneless, skinless chicken thighs, diced
- 1 lb smoked sausage, sliced
- 1 onion, chopped
- 1 bell pepper, chopped
- 2 celery stalks, chopped
- 4 cups chicken broth
- 1 can (14 oz) diced tomatoes
- 2 tablespoons Cajun seasoning
- Cooked rice for serving

Instructions:

1. In a large pot, brown sausage over medium heat, then remove and set aside.
2. In the same pot, sauté onion, bell pepper, and celery until softened.
3. Add chicken, broth, tomatoes, and Cajun seasoning, then bring to a boil.
4. Reduce heat and simmer for 30 minutes, adding sausage back in for the last 10 minutes.
5. Serve over cooked rice.

Pesto Chicken Pasta Salad

Ingredients:

- 2 cups cooked pasta (penne or rotini)
- 1 cup cooked chicken, diced
- 1/2 cup pesto sauce
- 1 cup cherry tomatoes, halved
- 1/2 cup mozzarella balls, halved
- Salt and pepper to taste
- Fresh basil for garnish

Instructions:

1. In a large bowl, combine cooked pasta, chicken, pesto sauce, cherry tomatoes, and mozzarella.
2. Toss gently to combine, seasoning with salt and pepper.
3. Garnish with fresh basil before serving.

Chicken Cacciatore with Bell Peppers

Ingredients:

- 4 chicken thighs, bone-in
- 1 onion, sliced
- 1 bell pepper, sliced
- 2 cloves garlic, minced
- 1 can (14 oz) diced tomatoes
- 1/2 cup chicken broth
- 1 teaspoon Italian seasoning
- Salt and pepper to taste

Instructions:

1. In a large skillet, brown chicken thighs on both sides.
2. Remove chicken and sauté onion, bell pepper, and garlic until softened.
3. Add tomatoes, chicken broth, Italian seasoning, salt, and pepper.
4. Return chicken to the skillet, cover, and simmer for 30-40 minutes until cooked through.

Sesame Chicken with Broccoli

Ingredients:

- 1 lb chicken breast, cubed
- 2 cups broccoli florets
- 1/4 cup soy sauce
- 2 tablespoons sesame oil
- 2 tablespoons honey
- 2 tablespoons sesame seeds
- 2 cloves garlic, minced

Instructions:

1. In a bowl, mix soy sauce, sesame oil, honey, and garlic.
2. Marinate chicken in the mixture for 30 minutes.
3. In a large skillet, cook marinated chicken until browned.
4. Add broccoli and cook until tender, about 5 minutes.
5. Sprinkle with sesame seeds before serving.

Stuffed Chicken Breasts with Sun-Dried Tomatoes

Ingredients:

- 4 boneless, skinless chicken breasts
- 1/2 cup sun-dried tomatoes, chopped
- 1/2 cup feta cheese, crumbled
- 1 cup spinach, chopped
- 1 tablespoon olive oil
- Salt and pepper to taste

Instructions:

1. Preheat oven to 375°F (190°C).
2. In a bowl, mix sun-dried tomatoes, feta, and spinach.
3. Cut a pocket in each chicken breast and fill with the mixture.
4. Heat olive oil in a skillet and sear chicken on both sides.
5. Transfer to a baking dish and bake for 25-30 minutes until cooked through.

Chicken and Vegetable Stir-Fry

Ingredients:

- 1 lb chicken breast, sliced
- 2 cups mixed vegetables (bell peppers, broccoli, carrots)
- 1/4 cup soy sauce
- 2 tablespoons vegetable oil
- 2 cloves garlic, minced
- 1 teaspoon ginger, minced

Instructions:

1. Heat oil in a large skillet or wok over medium-high heat.
2. Add chicken and cook until browned.
3. Add garlic, ginger, and mixed vegetables, stir-frying until vegetables are tender.
4. Stir in soy sauce and cook for an additional 2 minutes before serving.

Chipotle Chicken Burrito Bowl

Ingredients:

- 1 lb chicken breast, grilled and sliced
- 2 cups cooked rice (white or brown)
- 1 can (15 oz) black beans, rinsed and drained
- 1 cup corn, cooked
- 1 avocado, diced
- 1/4 cup chipotle sauce
- Lime wedges for serving

Instructions:

1. In a bowl, layer rice, black beans, corn, grilled chicken, and avocado.
2. Drizzle chipotle sauce on top and serve with lime wedges.

Thai Basil Chicken

Ingredients:

- 1 lb chicken breast, ground
- 1 cup fresh basil leaves
- 1/4 cup soy sauce
- 2 tablespoons fish sauce
- 1 tablespoon sugar
- 2 cloves garlic, minced
- 1-2 Thai chilies, sliced (optional)

Instructions:

1. In a skillet, cook garlic until fragrant, then add ground chicken.
2. Cook until chicken is browned.
3. Stir in soy sauce, fish sauce, sugar, and chilies.
4. Add basil leaves and cook until wilted before serving.

Creamy Tuscan Chicken

Ingredients:

- 4 chicken breasts
- 1 cup heavy cream
- 1/2 cup sun-dried tomatoes, chopped
- 1 cup spinach, chopped
- 2 cloves garlic, minced
- 1 teaspoon Italian seasoning
- Salt and pepper to taste

Instructions:

1. In a skillet, cook chicken breasts until browned and cooked through.
2. Remove chicken and sauté garlic in the same skillet.
3. Add sun-dried tomatoes, cream, Italian seasoning, salt, and pepper.
4. Stir in spinach and cook until wilted, then return chicken to the skillet to coat in sauce before serving.

Buttermilk Fried Chicken

Ingredients:

- 4 chicken pieces (legs, thighs, or breasts)
- 2 cups buttermilk
- 1 cup all-purpose flour
- 1 teaspoon paprika
- 1 teaspoon garlic powder
- Salt and pepper to taste
- Oil for frying

Instructions:

1. **Marinate**: Place chicken in a bowl and cover with buttermilk. Refrigerate for at least 4 hours or overnight.
2. **Prepare Coating**: In a separate bowl, mix flour, paprika, garlic powder, salt, and pepper.
3. **Coat Chicken**: Remove chicken from buttermilk, allowing excess to drip off. Dredge in flour mixture until fully coated.
4. **Fry**: Heat oil in a large skillet over medium-high heat. Fry chicken pieces until golden brown and cooked through, about 10-15 minutes per side. Drain on paper towels before serving.

Chicken Pot Pie with Flaky Crust

Ingredients:

- 2 cups cooked chicken, diced
- 1 cup carrots, diced
- 1 cup peas
- 1/2 cup celery, diced
- 1/3 cup butter
- 1/3 cup all-purpose flour
- 1 cup chicken broth
- 1 cup milk
- Salt and pepper to taste
- 1 refrigerated pie crust

Instructions:

1. **Preheat Oven**: Preheat oven to 425°F (220°C).
2. **Cook Vegetables**: In a saucepan, melt butter over medium heat. Add carrots, peas, and celery. Cook until tender.
3. **Make Sauce**: Stir in flour and cook for 1 minute. Gradually add chicken broth and milk, stirring until thickened. Season with salt and pepper.
4. **Combine**: Stir in cooked chicken.
5. **Assemble Pie**: Pour mixture into a pie crust in a pie pan. Top with another crust, seal edges, and cut slits in the top for steam to escape.
6. **Bake**: Bake for 30-35 minutes until crust is golden brown. Let cool before serving.

Maple-Mustard Glazed Chicken

Ingredients:

- 4 chicken breasts
- 1/4 cup maple syrup
- 2 tablespoons Dijon mustard
- 1 tablespoon olive oil
- Salt and pepper to taste

Instructions:

1. **Preheat Oven**: Preheat oven to 375°F (190°C).
2. **Make Glaze**: In a bowl, whisk together maple syrup, Dijon mustard, olive oil, salt, and pepper.
3. **Coat Chicken**: Place chicken breasts in a baking dish and pour glaze over the top.
4. **Bake**: Bake for 25-30 minutes or until chicken is cooked through and juices run clear. Brush with additional glaze halfway through cooking.

Chicken Roulade with Spinach and Ricotta

Ingredients:

- 4 chicken breasts, butterflied
- 1 cup ricotta cheese
- 1 cup spinach, cooked and chopped
- 1/2 cup Parmesan cheese, grated
- Salt and pepper to taste
- Olive oil for drizzling

Instructions:

1. **Preheat Oven**: Preheat oven to 375°F (190°C).
2. **Prepare Filling**: In a bowl, mix ricotta, spinach, Parmesan, salt, and pepper.
3. **Assemble Roulades**: Spread filling on each chicken breast, roll up tightly, and secure with toothpicks.
4. **Bake**: Place roulades in a baking dish, drizzle with olive oil, and bake for 25-30 minutes or until cooked through. Remove toothpicks before serving.

Chicken Caesar Salad with Homemade Dressing

Ingredients:

- 2 cups romaine lettuce, chopped
- 1 cup cooked chicken, sliced
- 1/4 cup Parmesan cheese, grated
- Croutons
- 1/4 cup mayonnaise
- 1 tablespoon Dijon mustard
- 1 tablespoon lemon juice
- 1 clove garlic, minced
- Salt and pepper to taste

Instructions:

1. **Make Dressing**: In a bowl, whisk together mayonnaise, Dijon mustard, lemon juice, garlic, salt, and pepper.
2. **Combine Salad**: In a large bowl, combine romaine, chicken, and croutons.
3. **Toss**: Drizzle dressing over the salad and toss to combine. Top with Parmesan cheese before serving.

Garlic Parmesan Chicken Wings

Ingredients:

- 2 lbs chicken wings
- 1/4 cup butter, melted
- 4 cloves garlic, minced
- 1/2 cup Parmesan cheese, grated
- 1 teaspoon Italian seasoning
- Salt and pepper to taste

Instructions:

1. **Preheat Oven**: Preheat oven to 400°F (200°C).
2. **Prepare Wings**: Place wings in a baking dish and season with salt and pepper.
3. **Make Sauce**: In a bowl, mix melted butter, garlic, Parmesan, and Italian seasoning. Pour over wings, tossing to coat.
4. **Bake**: Bake for 40-45 minutes, turning halfway, until crispy and golden.

Chicken and Spinach Stuffed Shells

Ingredients:

- 12 jumbo pasta shells, cooked
- 1 cup cooked chicken, shredded
- 1 cup spinach, cooked and chopped
- 1 cup ricotta cheese
- 1 cup marinara sauce
- 1/2 cup mozzarella cheese, shredded
- Salt and pepper to taste

Instructions:

1. **Preheat Oven**: Preheat oven to 375°F (190°C).
2. **Prepare Filling**: In a bowl, mix chicken, spinach, ricotta, salt, and pepper.
3. **Stuff Shells**: Fill each pasta shell with the chicken mixture and place in a baking dish.
4. **Add Sauce**: Pour marinara sauce over the shells and sprinkle with mozzarella cheese.
5. **Bake**: Bake for 20-25 minutes until heated through and cheese is bubbly.

Cajun Chicken Pasta

Ingredients:

- 2 chicken breasts, sliced
- 8 oz penne pasta, cooked
- 1 bell pepper, sliced
- 1 onion, sliced
- 1 cup heavy cream
- 2 tablespoons Cajun seasoning
- 2 tablespoons olive oil
- Salt and pepper to taste

Instructions:

1. **Cook Chicken**: In a skillet, heat olive oil and cook chicken until browned. Season with Cajun seasoning.
2. **Add Vegetables**: Add bell pepper and onion, cooking until softened.
3. **Combine Pasta**: Stir in heavy cream and cooked pasta, mixing to combine. Season with salt and pepper before serving.

Chicken and Broccoli Alfredo Bake

Ingredients:

- 2 cups cooked chicken, shredded
- 2 cups broccoli florets, steamed
- 12 oz fettuccine, cooked
- 2 cups Alfredo sauce
- 1 cup shredded mozzarella cheese
- 1/2 cup grated Parmesan cheese
- Salt and pepper to taste

Instructions:

1. **Preheat Oven**: Preheat oven to 350°F (175°C).
2. **Combine Ingredients**: In a large bowl, mix cooked chicken, broccoli, fettuccine, Alfredo sauce, salt, and pepper until well combined.
3. **Transfer to Baking Dish**: Pour mixture into a greased baking dish and sprinkle mozzarella and Parmesan cheese on top.
4. **Bake**: Bake for 25-30 minutes until bubbly and cheese is golden.

Lemon Garlic Herb Chicken Thighs

Ingredients:

- 4 chicken thighs, skin-on
- 3 cloves garlic, minced
- Juice of 1 lemon
- 2 tablespoons olive oil
- 1 teaspoon dried thyme
- 1 teaspoon dried rosemary
- Salt and pepper to taste

Instructions:

1. **Preheat Oven**: Preheat oven to 400°F (200°C).
2. **Prepare Marinade**: In a bowl, whisk together garlic, lemon juice, olive oil, thyme, rosemary, salt, and pepper.
3. **Marinate Chicken**: Coat chicken thighs in the marinade and let sit for 30 minutes.
4. **Bake**: Place chicken in a baking dish and bake for 35-40 minutes until cooked through and skin is crispy.

Chicken Fajitas with Peppers and Onions

Ingredients:

- 2 chicken breasts, sliced
- 1 bell pepper, sliced
- 1 onion, sliced
- 2 tablespoons fajita seasoning
- 1 tablespoon olive oil
- Tortillas, for serving

Instructions:

1. **Cook Chicken**: In a large skillet, heat olive oil over medium-high heat. Add chicken and fajita seasoning, cooking until chicken is cooked through.
2. **Add Vegetables**: Stir in bell pepper and onion, cooking until softened.
3. **Serve**: Serve mixture in tortillas, garnished with your favorite toppings like salsa, guacamole, or sour cream.

Thai Chicken Satay with Peanut Sauce

Ingredients:

- 2 chicken breasts, cut into strips
- 1 tablespoon soy sauce
- 1 tablespoon curry powder
- 1 tablespoon brown sugar
- 1/4 cup coconut milk
- 1/2 cup peanut butter
- 1 tablespoon lime juice
- Skewers

Instructions:

1. **Marinate Chicken**: In a bowl, mix soy sauce, curry powder, brown sugar, and coconut milk. Add chicken and marinate for at least 30 minutes.
2. **Skewer Chicken**: Thread chicken onto skewers.
3. **Grill**: Grill skewers over medium heat for about 5-7 minutes on each side until cooked through.
4. **Make Peanut Sauce**: In a small bowl, mix peanut butter and lime juice until smooth. Serve with chicken skewers.

Chipotle Lime Grilled Chicken

Ingredients:

- 4 chicken breasts
- 2 tablespoons chipotle sauce
- Juice of 2 limes
- 2 tablespoons olive oil
- Salt and pepper to taste

Instructions:

1. **Marinate Chicken**: In a bowl, combine chipotle sauce, lime juice, olive oil, salt, and pepper. Add chicken and marinate for at least 1 hour.
2. **Preheat Grill**: Preheat grill to medium-high heat.
3. **Grill Chicken**: Grill chicken for 6-7 minutes per side or until cooked through. Let rest before slicing.

Orange-Glazed Chicken with Sesame Seeds

Ingredients:

- 4 chicken breasts
- 1 cup orange juice
- 1/4 cup soy sauce
- 2 tablespoons honey
- 1 tablespoon sesame oil
- Sesame seeds for garnish

Instructions:

1. **Make Glaze**: In a saucepan, combine orange juice, soy sauce, honey, and sesame oil. Simmer until thickened.
2. **Cook Chicken**: Season chicken with salt and pepper, and cook in a skillet over medium heat until browned and cooked through.
3. **Add Glaze**: Pour orange glaze over chicken, coating well. Serve garnished with sesame seeds.

Chicken and Quinoa Salad with Avocado

Ingredients:

- 2 cups cooked quinoa
- 2 chicken breasts, cooked and diced
- 1 avocado, diced
- 1 cup cherry tomatoes, halved
- 1/4 cup red onion, diced
- Juice of 1 lime
- Salt and pepper to taste

Instructions:

1. **Combine Ingredients**: In a large bowl, combine quinoa, chicken, avocado, cherry tomatoes, and red onion.
2. **Dress Salad**: Drizzle lime juice over salad and season with salt and pepper. Toss gently to combine.

Chicken Stroganoff with Egg Noodles

Ingredients:

- 2 chicken breasts, sliced
- 8 oz egg noodles, cooked
- 1 cup mushrooms, sliced
- 1/2 onion, diced
- 1 cup chicken broth
- 1/2 cup sour cream
- 2 tablespoons flour
- 2 tablespoons butter
- Salt and pepper to taste

Instructions:

1. **Cook Chicken**: In a skillet, melt butter and cook chicken until browned. Remove and set aside.
2. **Sauté Vegetables**: In the same skillet, sauté onion and mushrooms until tender.
3. **Make Sauce**: Sprinkle flour over vegetables, stir, and gradually add chicken broth. Cook until thickened.
4. **Combine**: Return chicken to skillet, stir in sour cream, and heat through. Serve over egg noodles.

Garlic and Herb Grilled Chicken Breasts

Ingredients:

- 4 chicken breasts
- 3 cloves garlic, minced
- 2 tablespoons olive oil
- 1 tablespoon fresh rosemary, chopped
- 1 tablespoon fresh thyme, chopped
- Juice of 1 lemon
- Salt and pepper to taste

Instructions:

1. **Prepare Marinade**: In a bowl, mix minced garlic, olive oil, rosemary, thyme, lemon juice, salt, and pepper.
2. **Marinate Chicken**: Place chicken breasts in a resealable bag or shallow dish, pouring the marinade over them. Seal and refrigerate for at least 1 hour, preferably overnight.
3. **Preheat Grill**: Preheat your grill to medium-high heat.
4. **Grill Chicken**: Remove chicken from the marinade and discard the excess. Grill chicken breasts for 6-7 minutes per side, or until the internal temperature reaches 165°F (75°C).
5. **Rest and Serve**: Let the chicken rest for a few minutes before slicing. Serve with your favorite sides.

www.ingramcontent.com/pod-product-compliance
Lightning Source LLC
LaVergne TN
LVHW081459060526
838201LV00056BA/2831